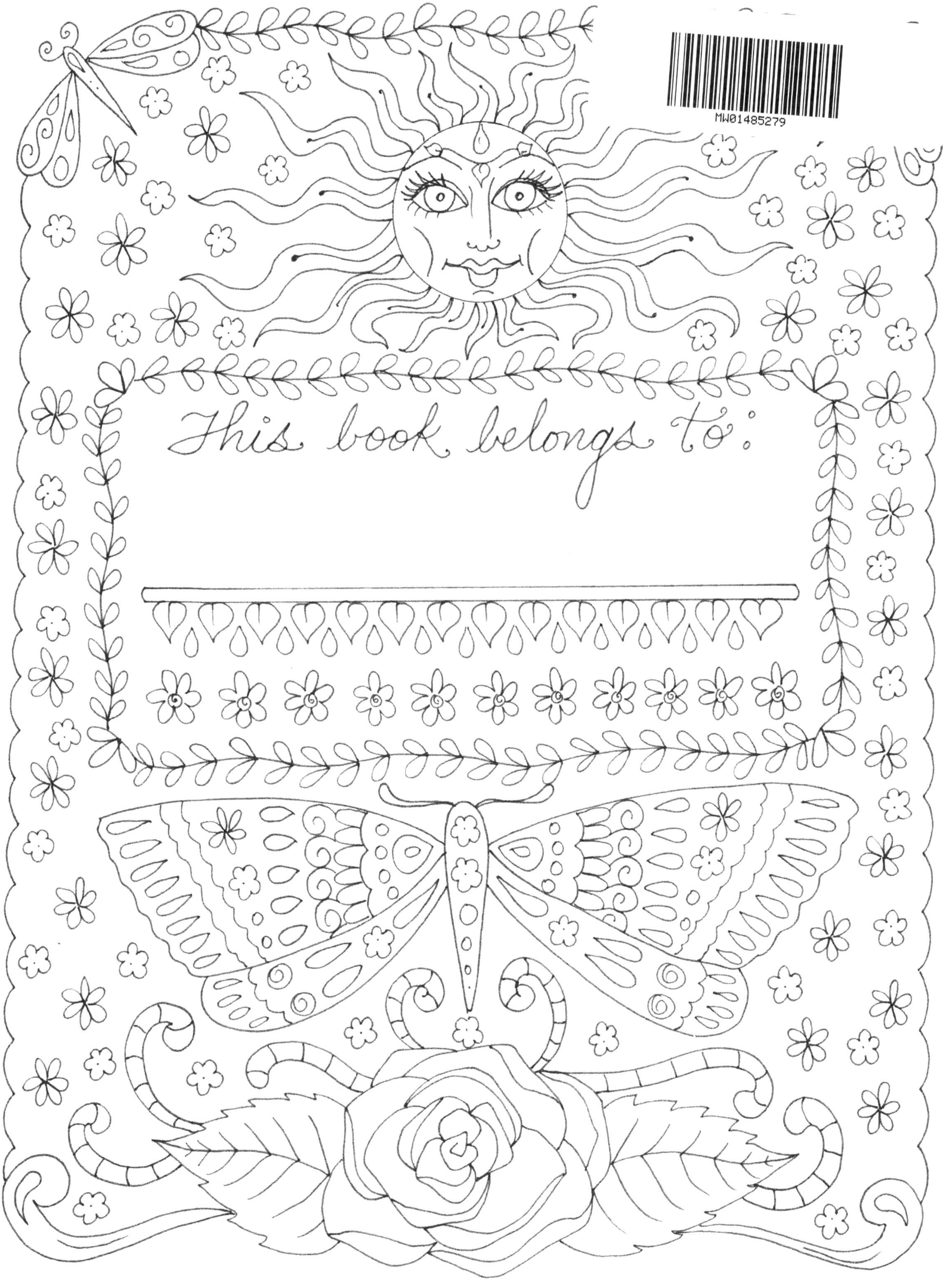
This book belongs to:

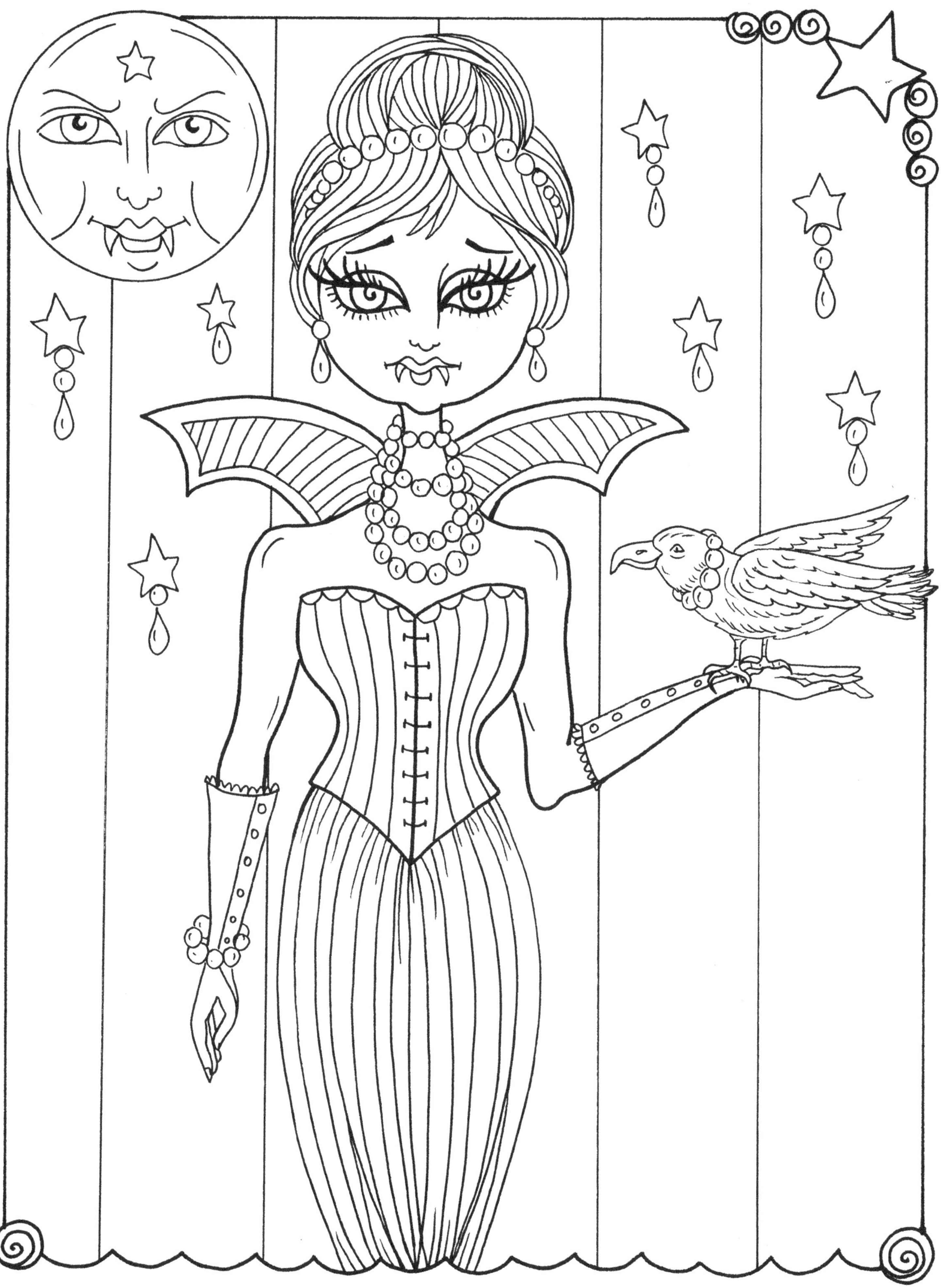

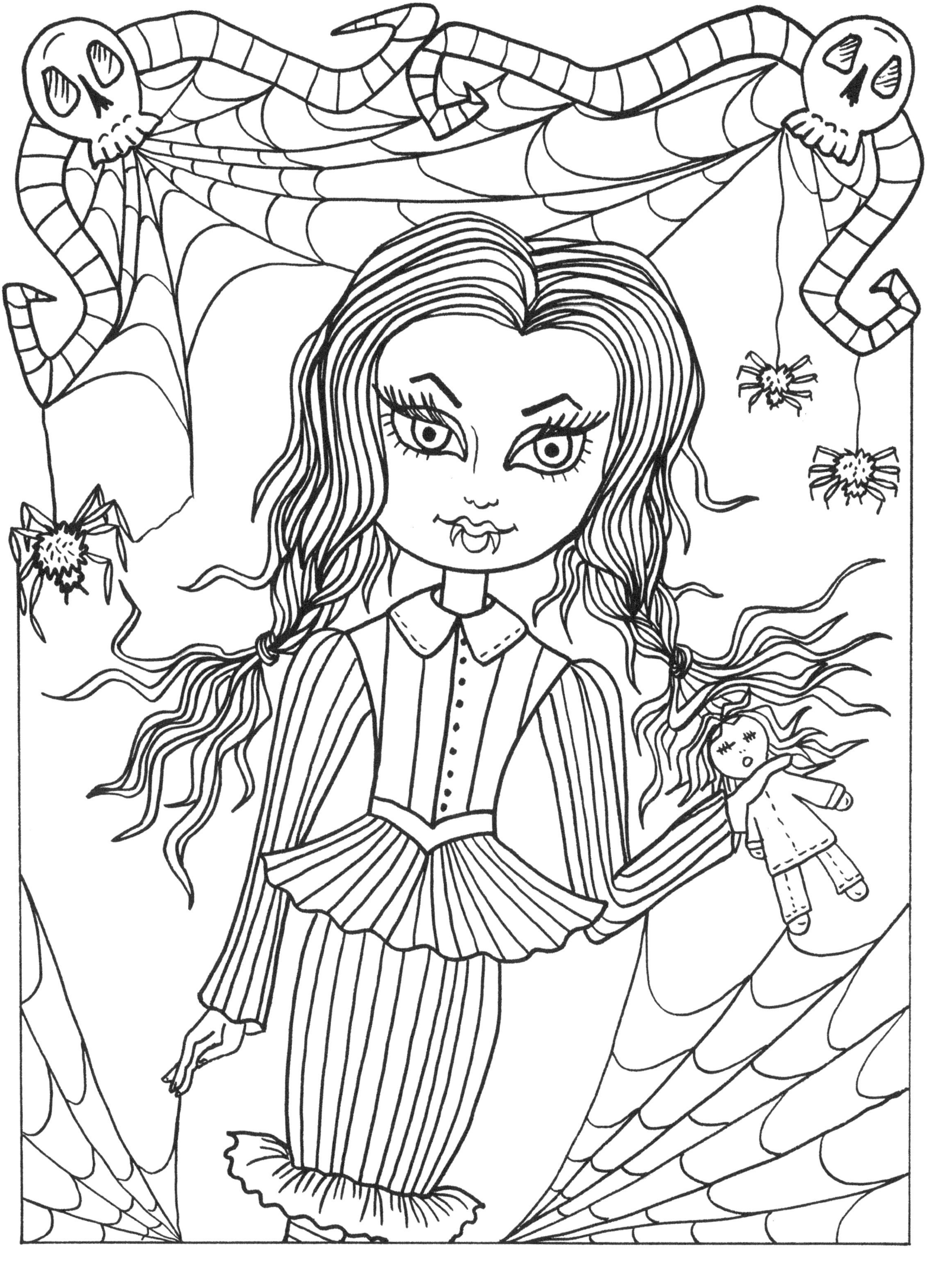

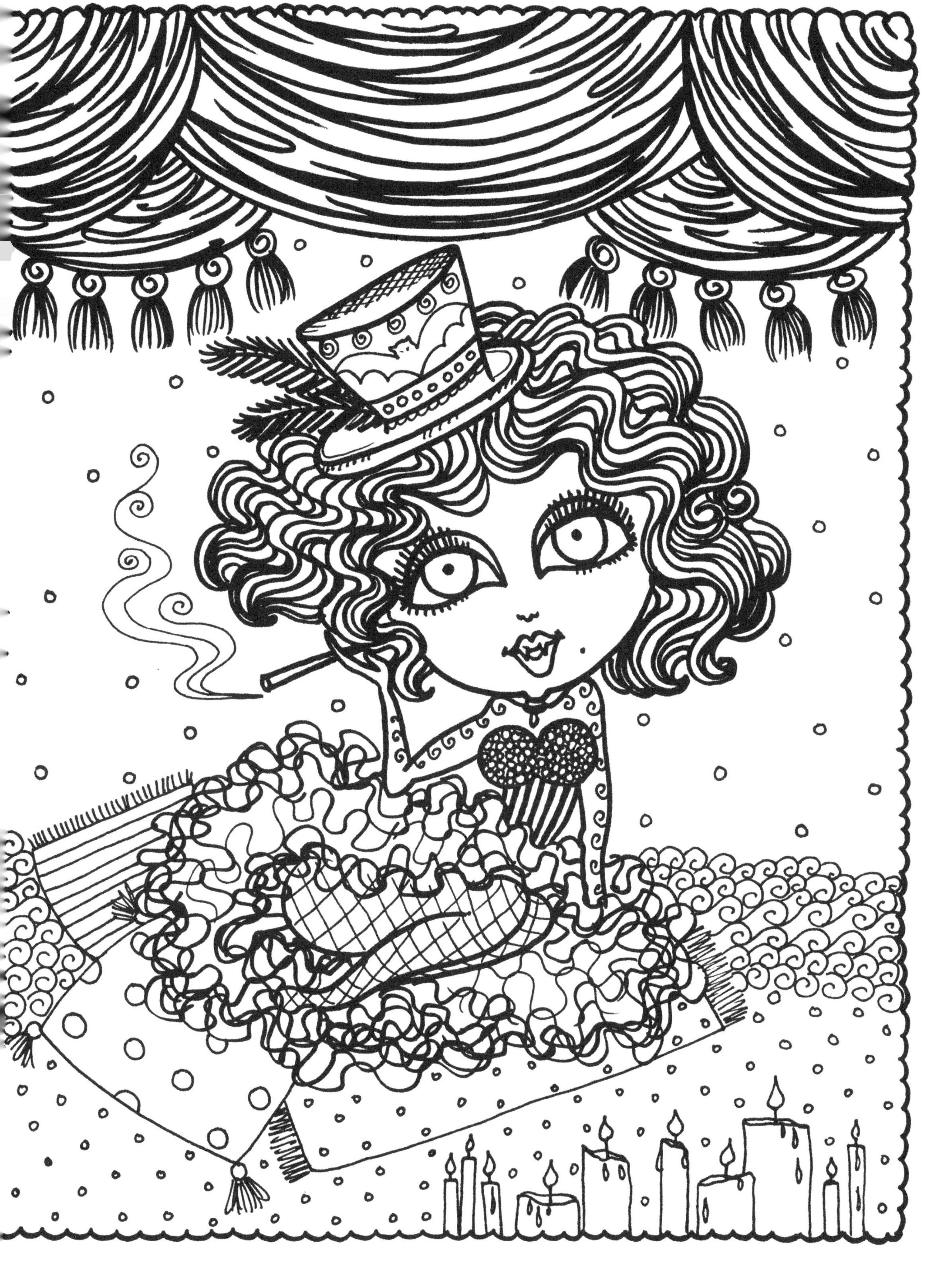

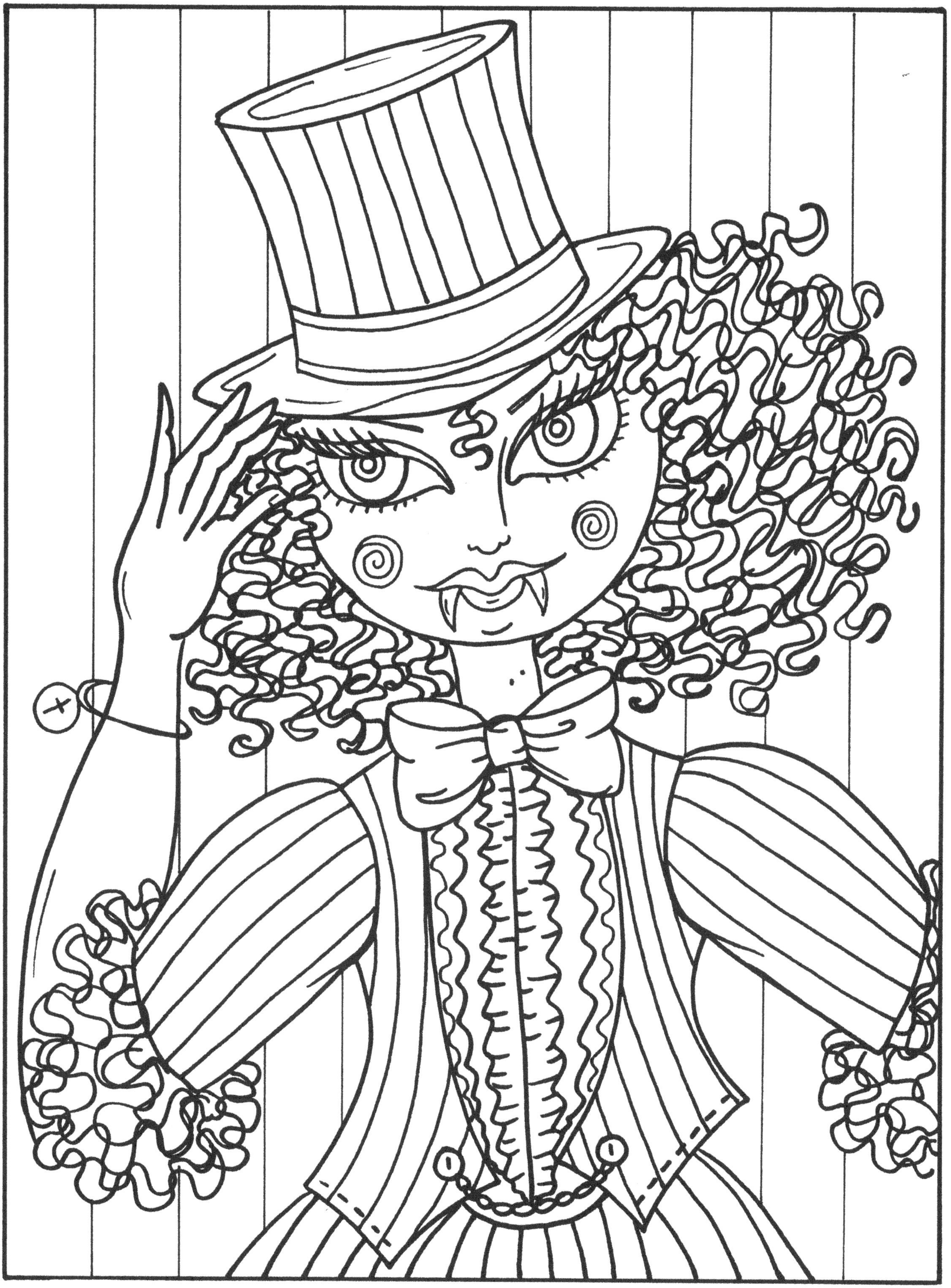

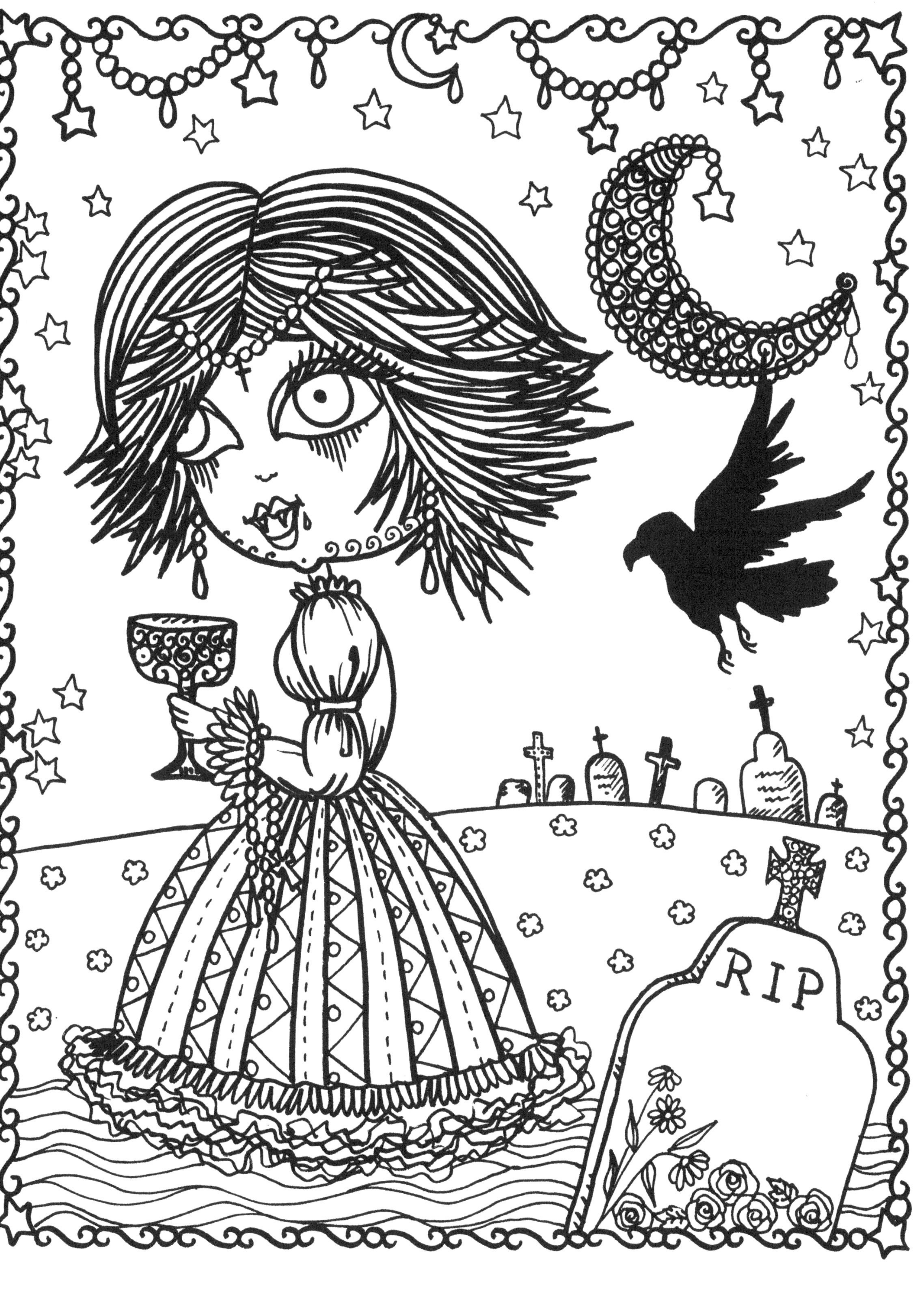
RIP

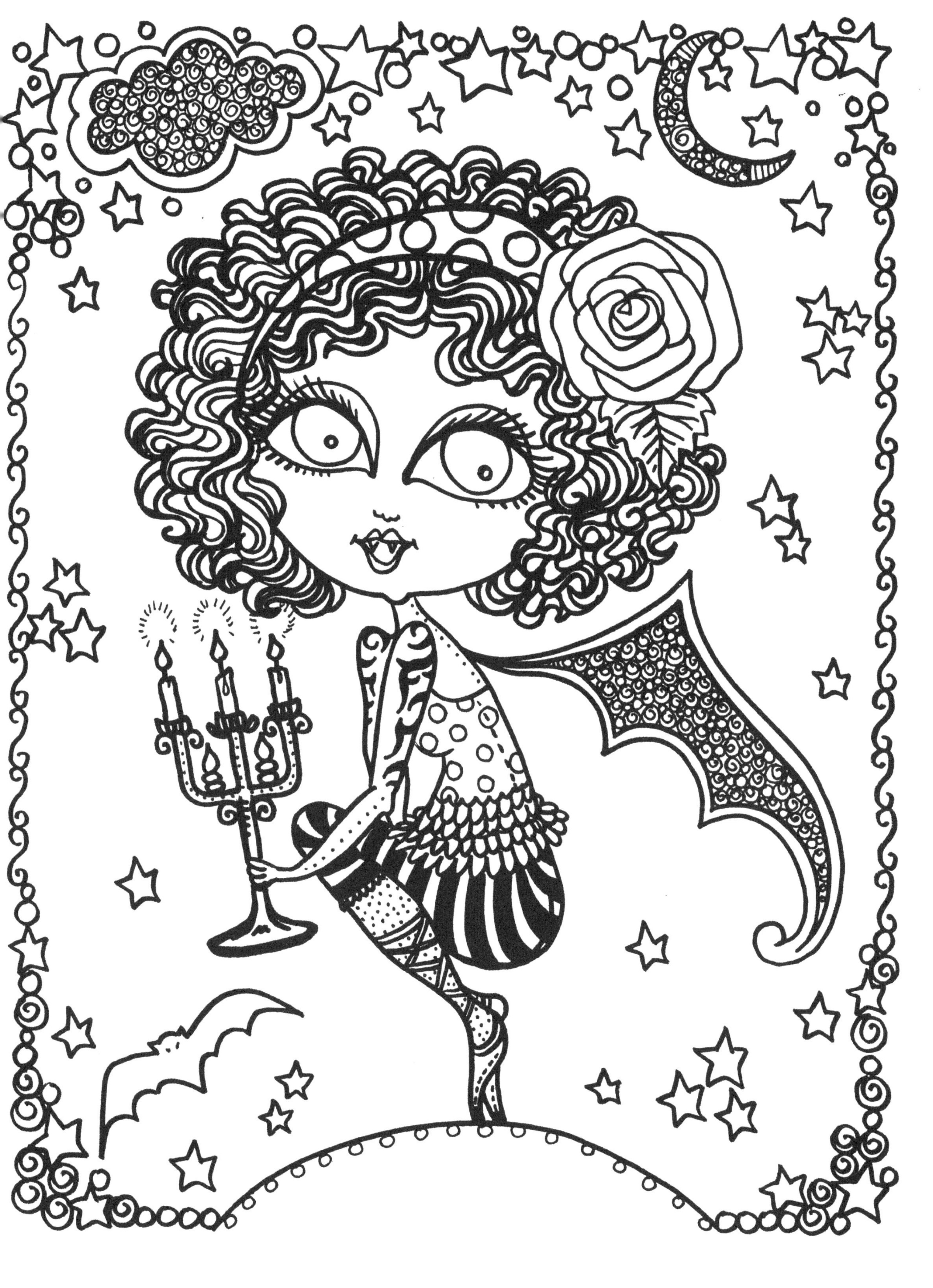

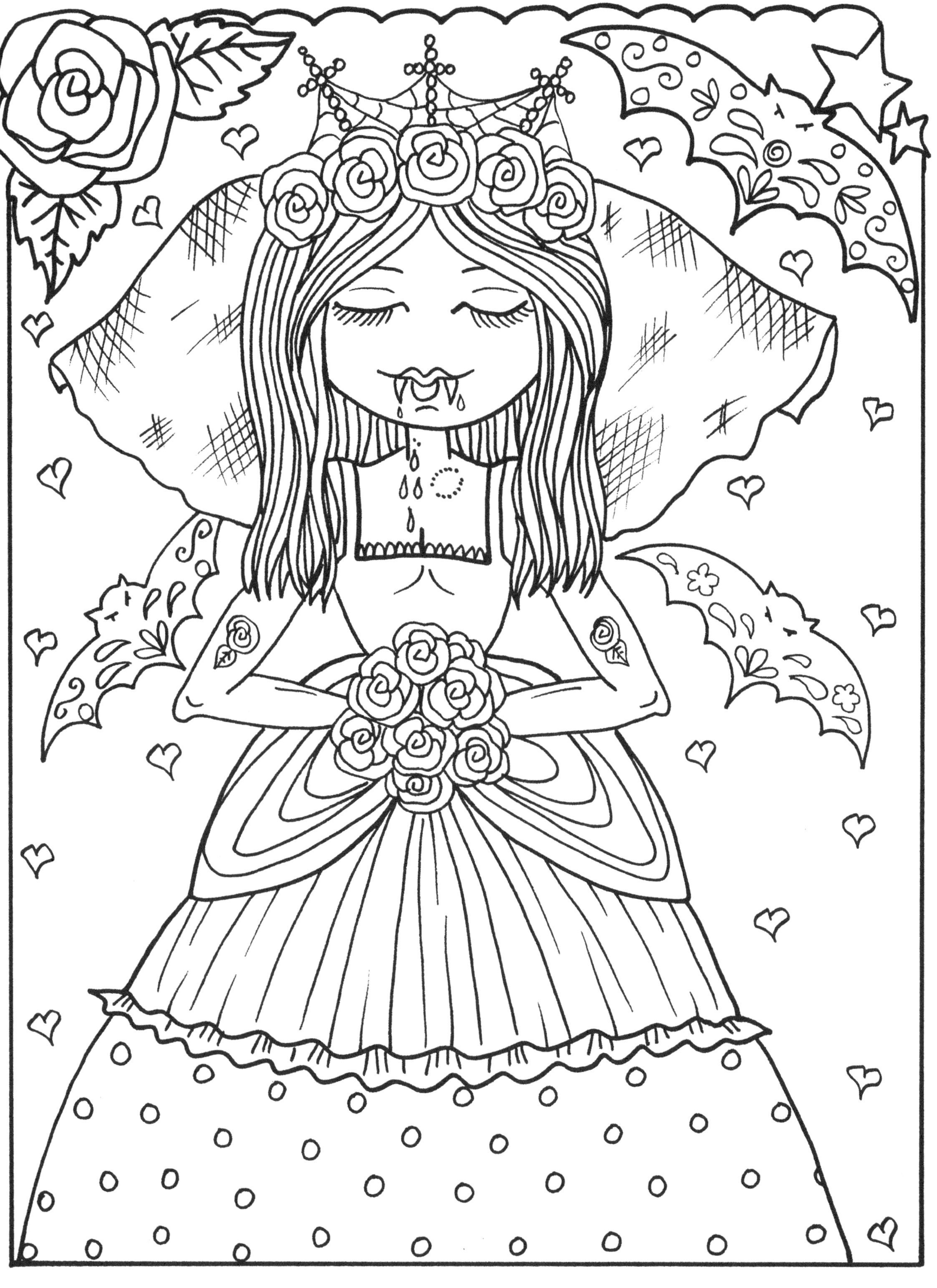

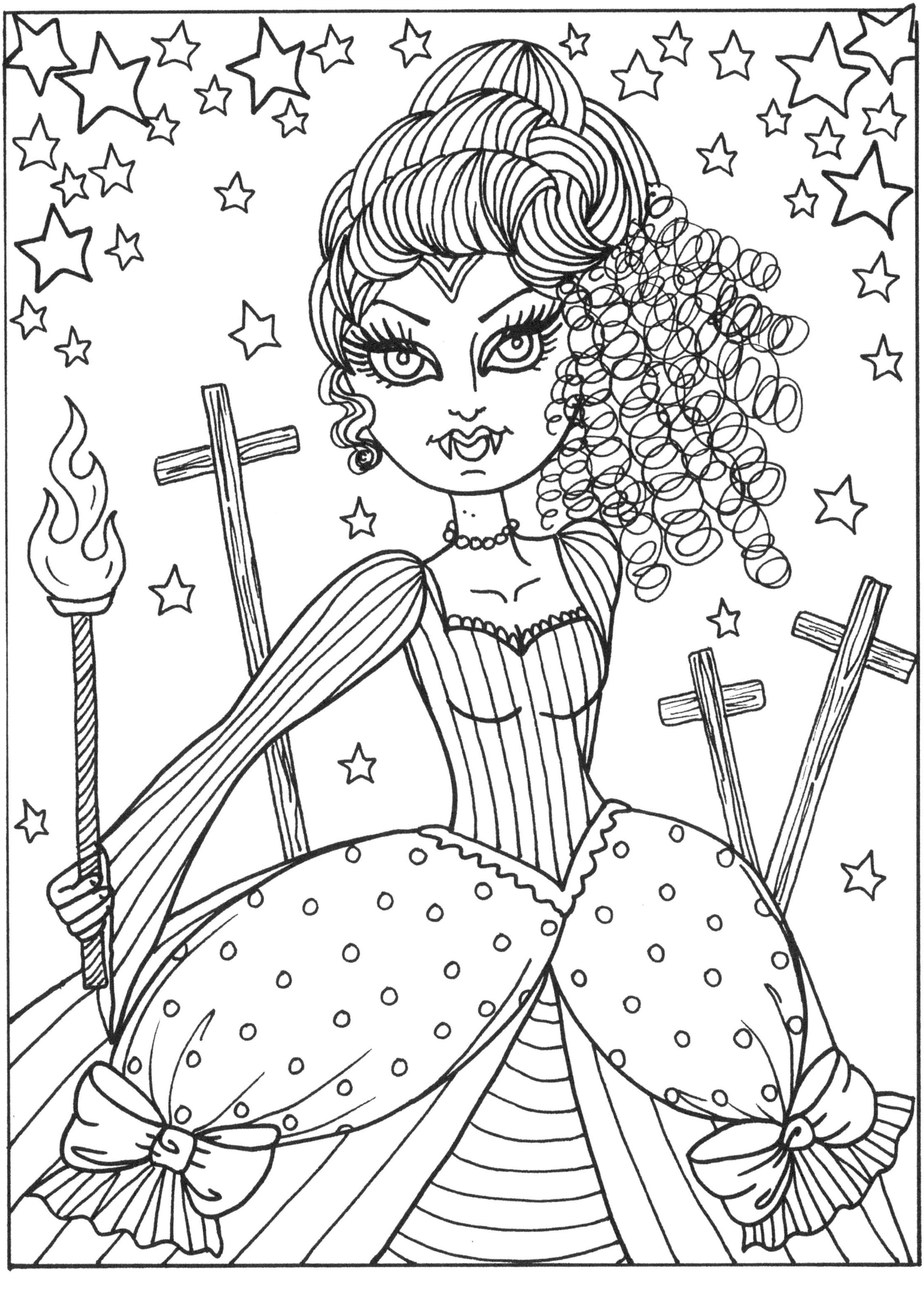

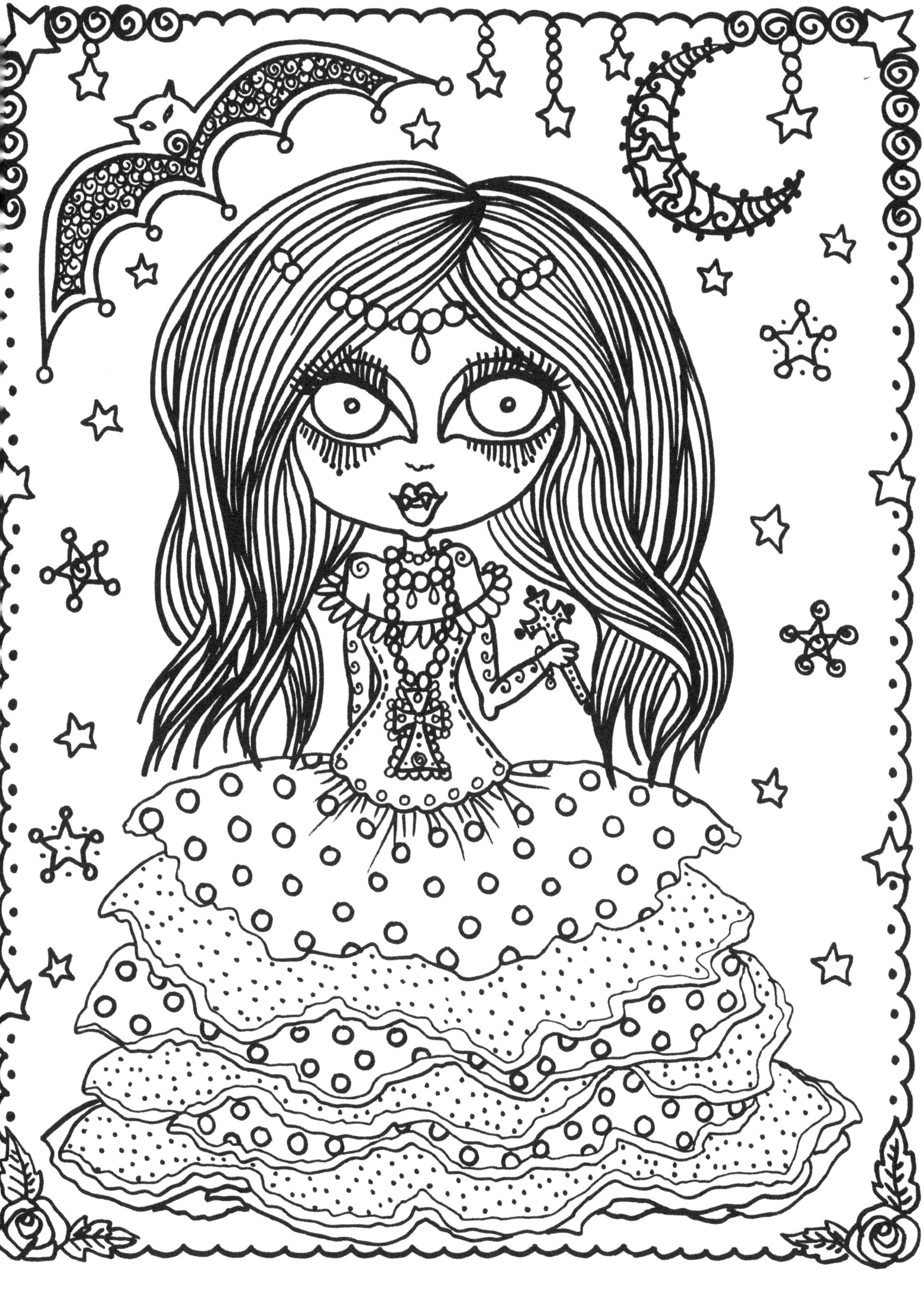

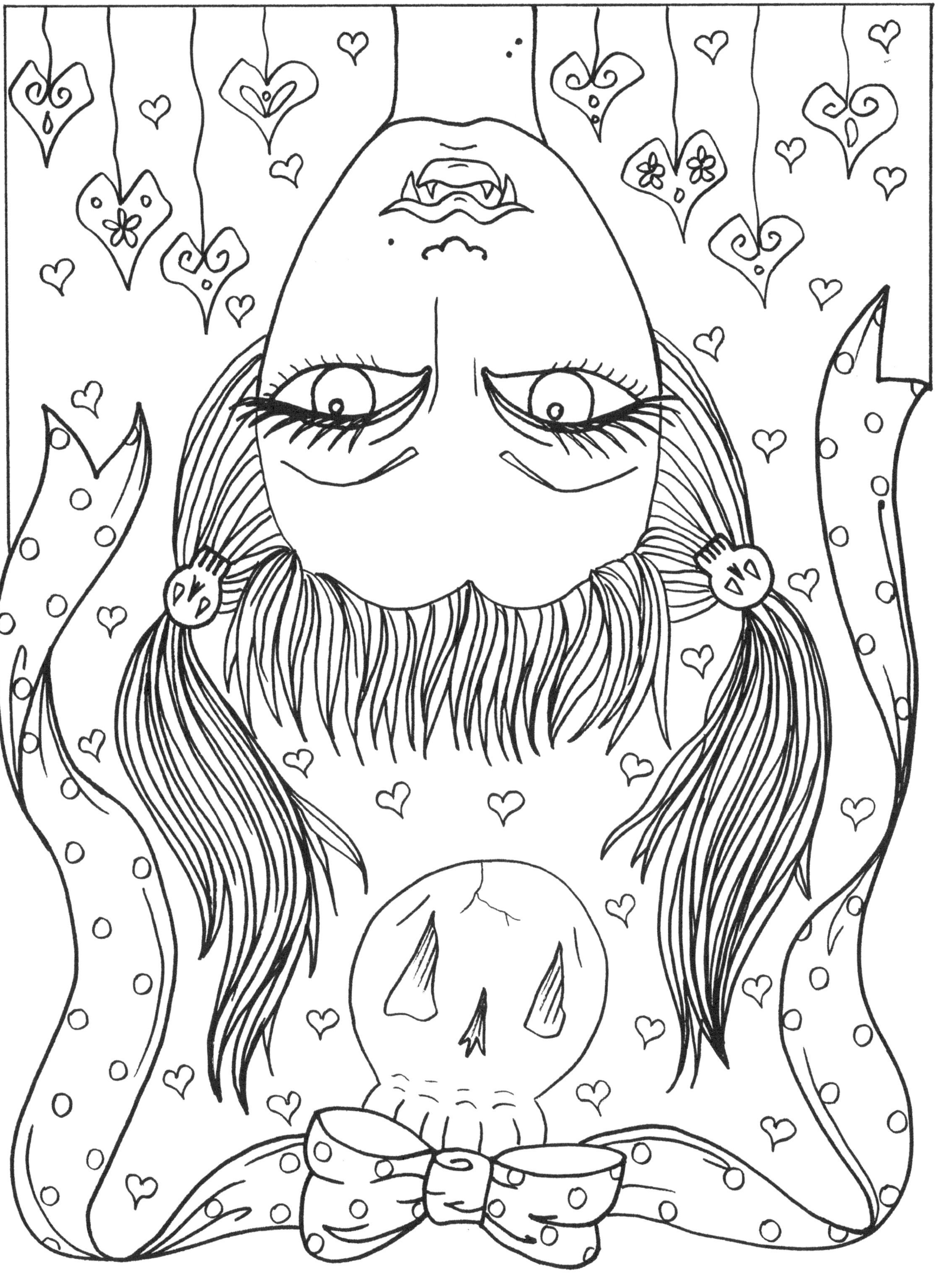

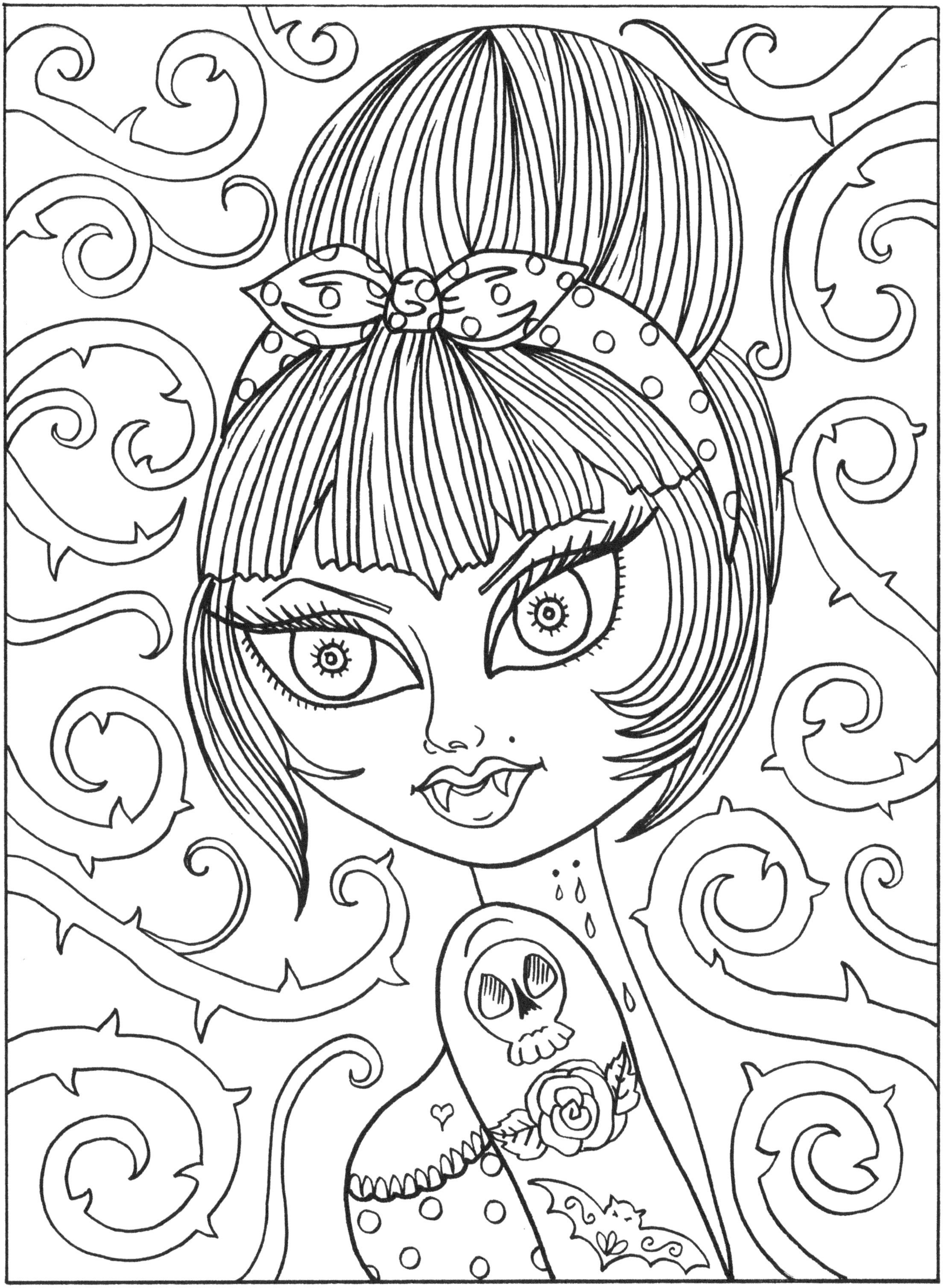

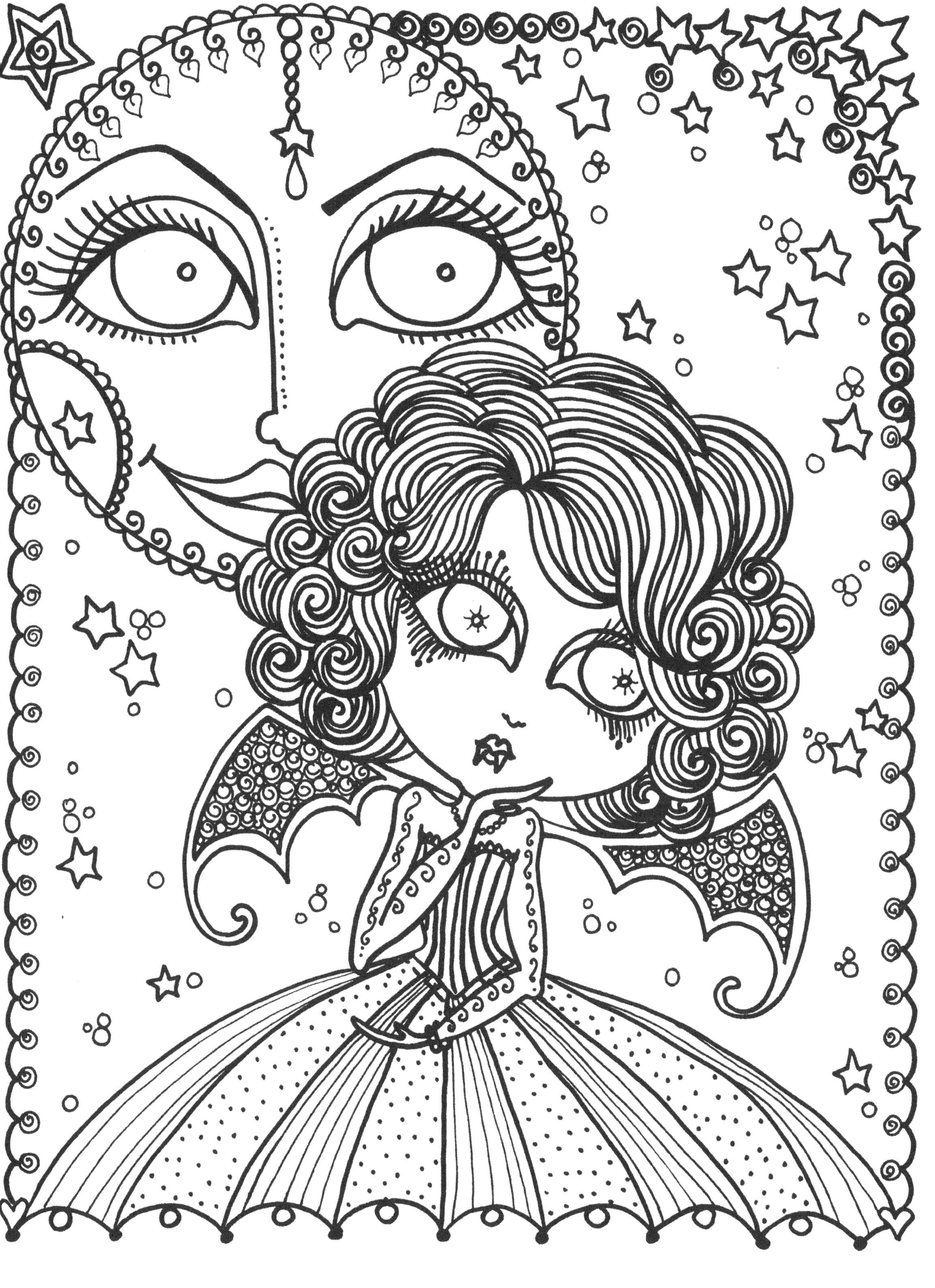

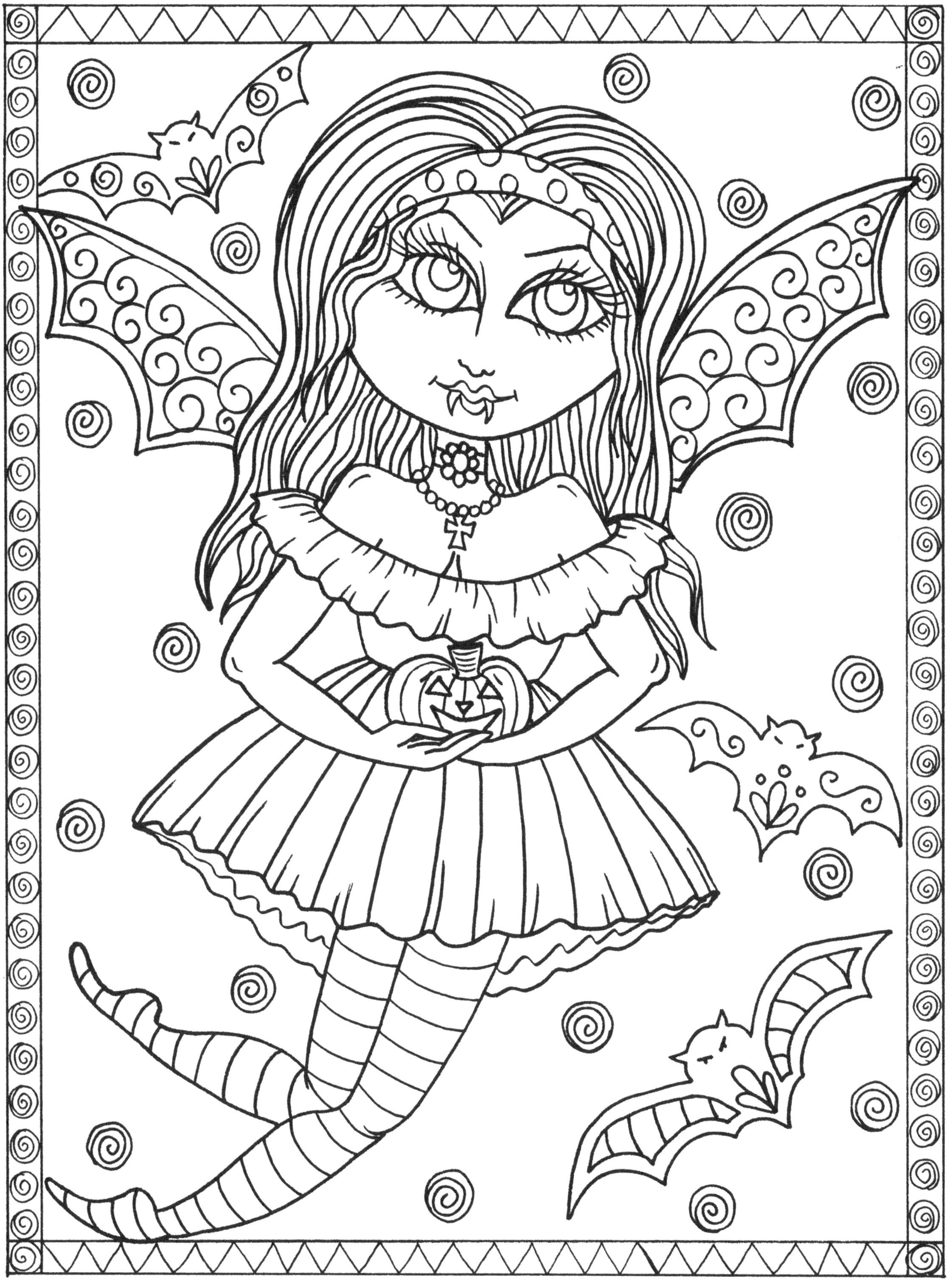

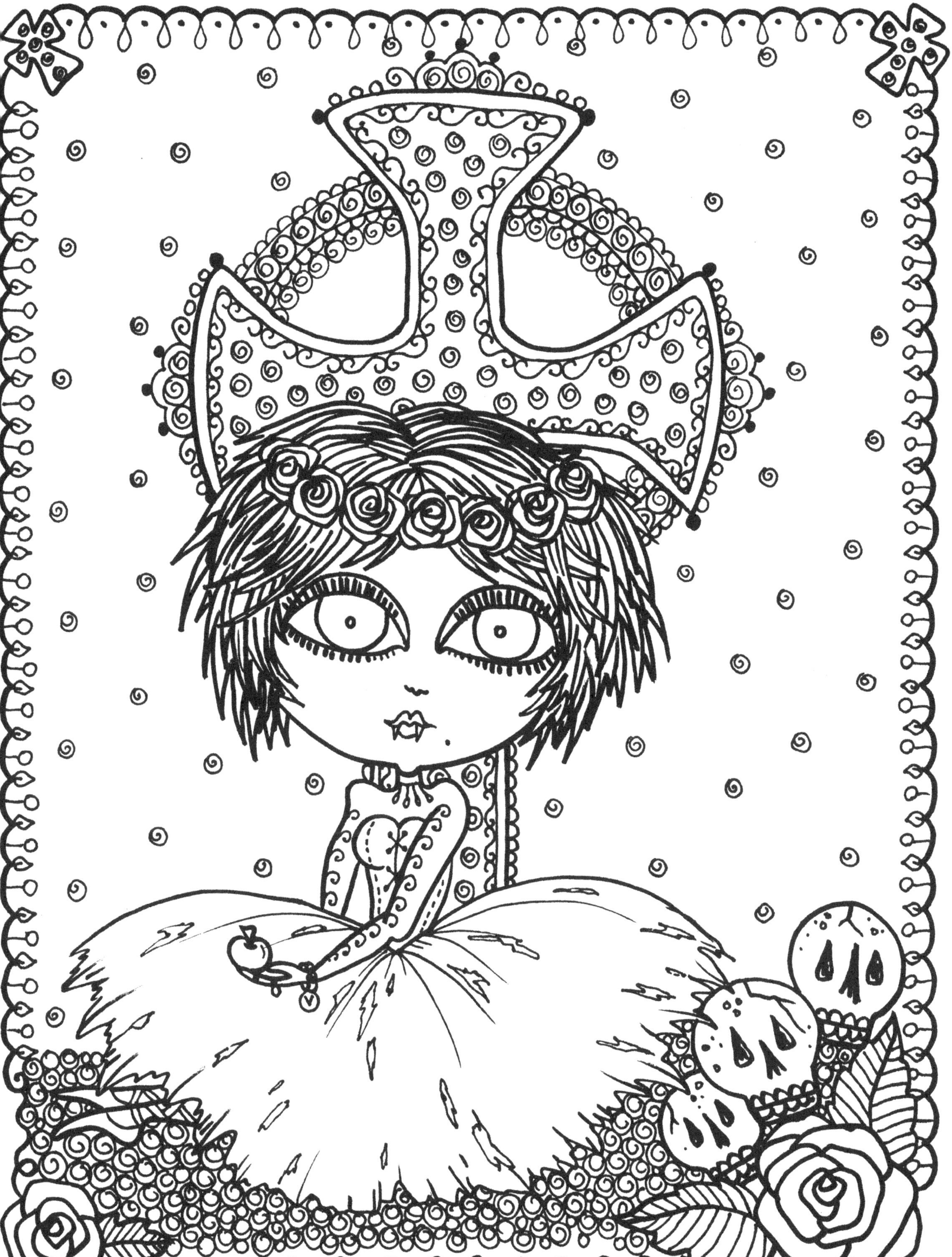

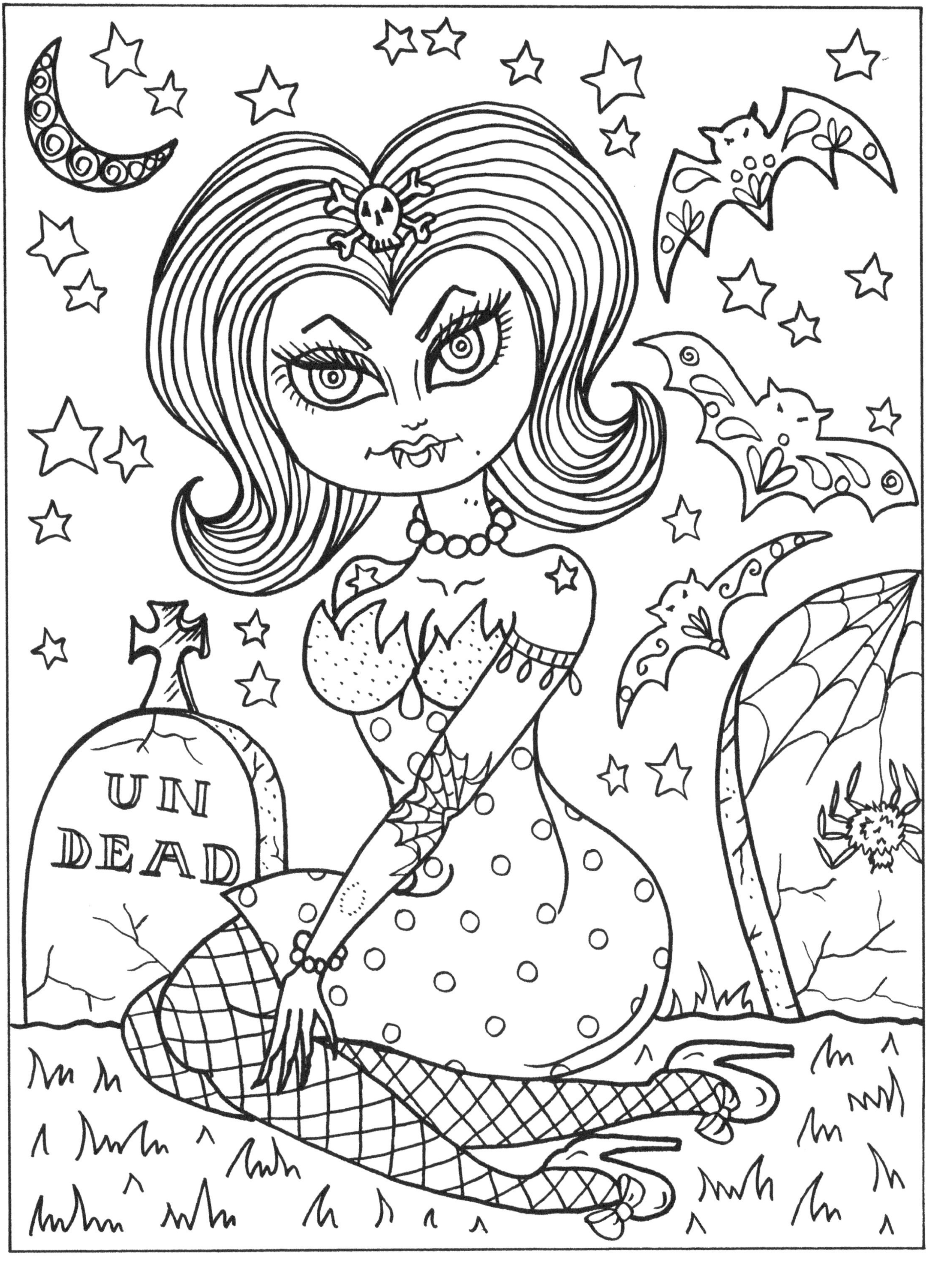
UN
DEAD

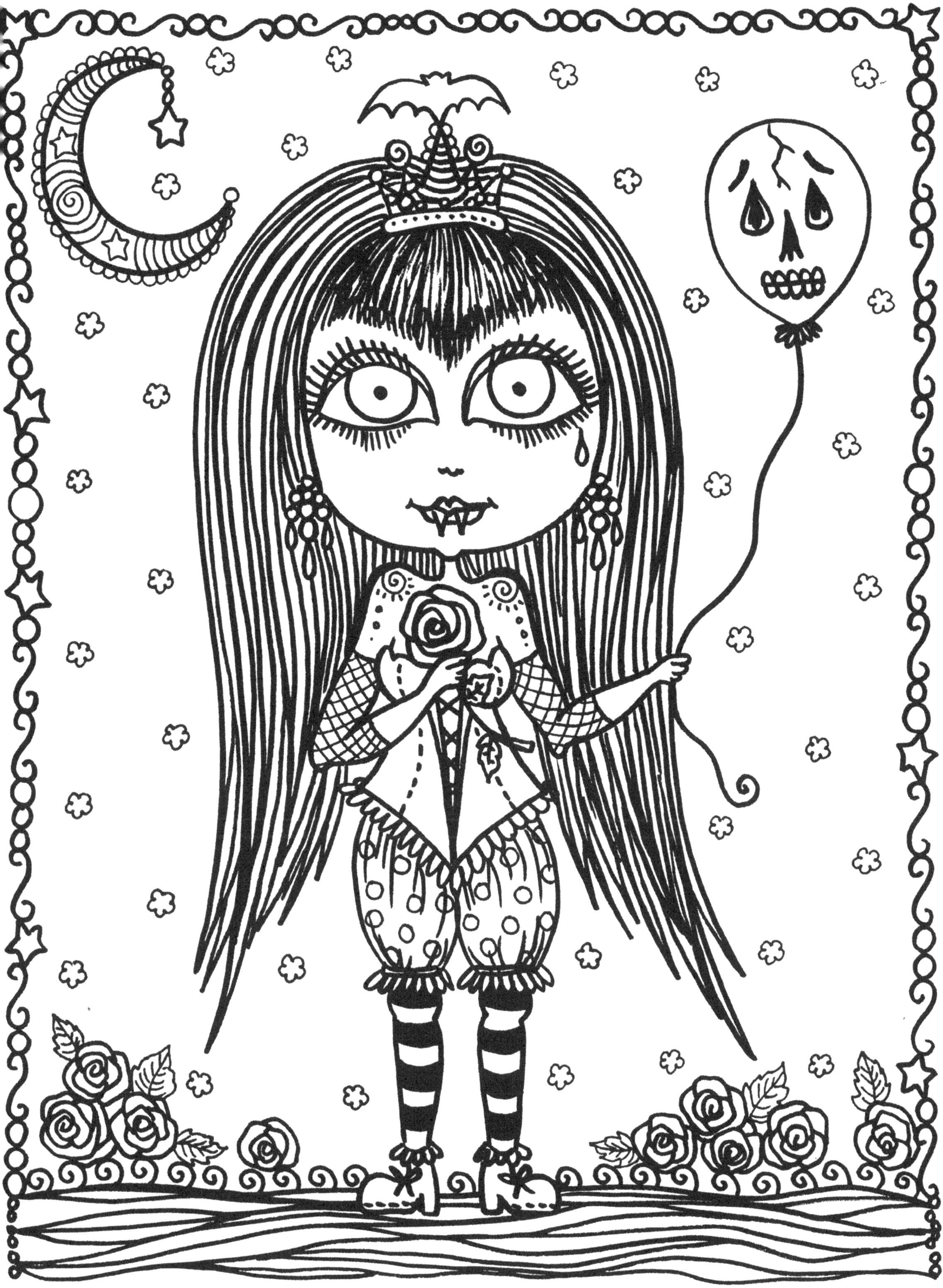

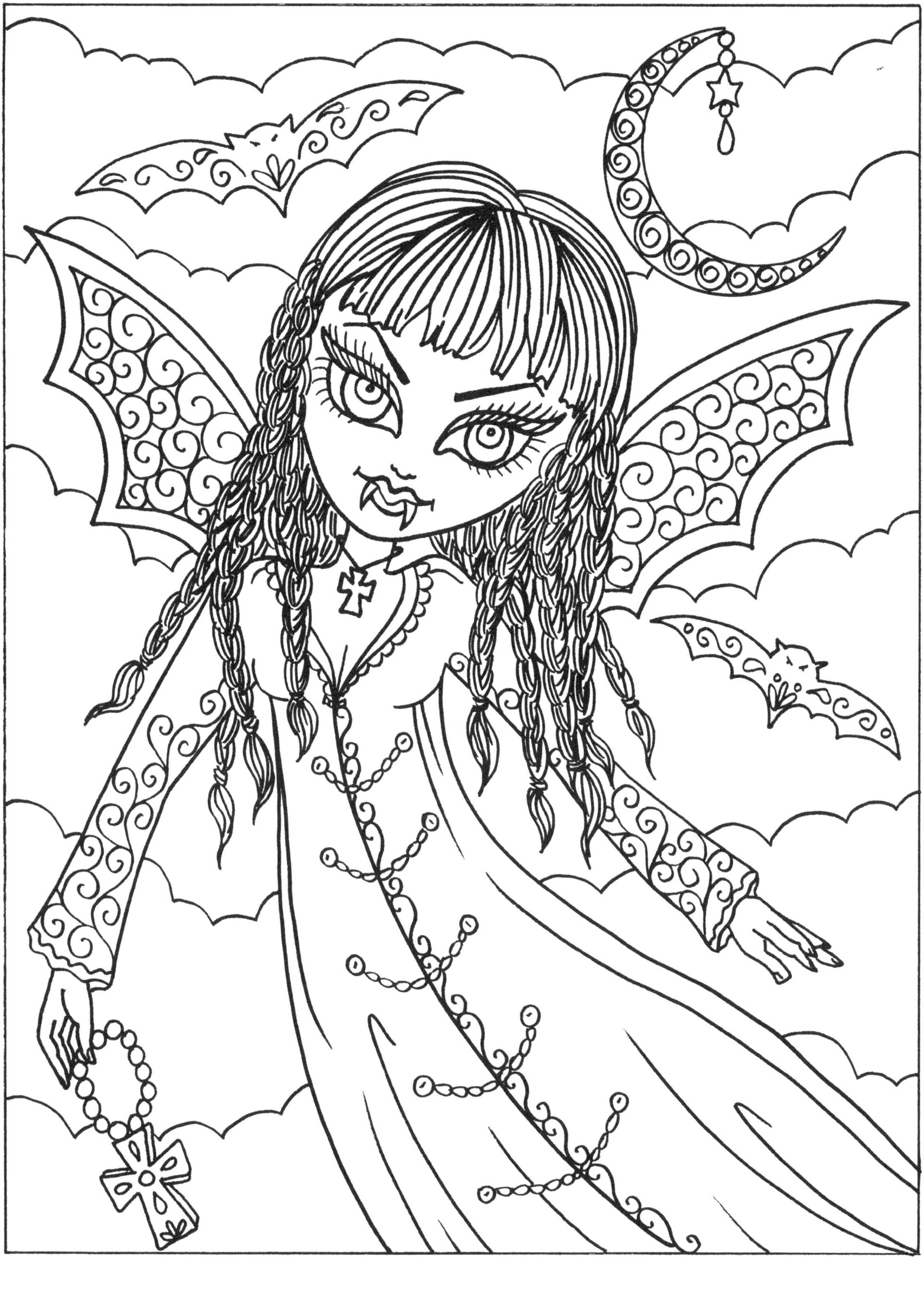

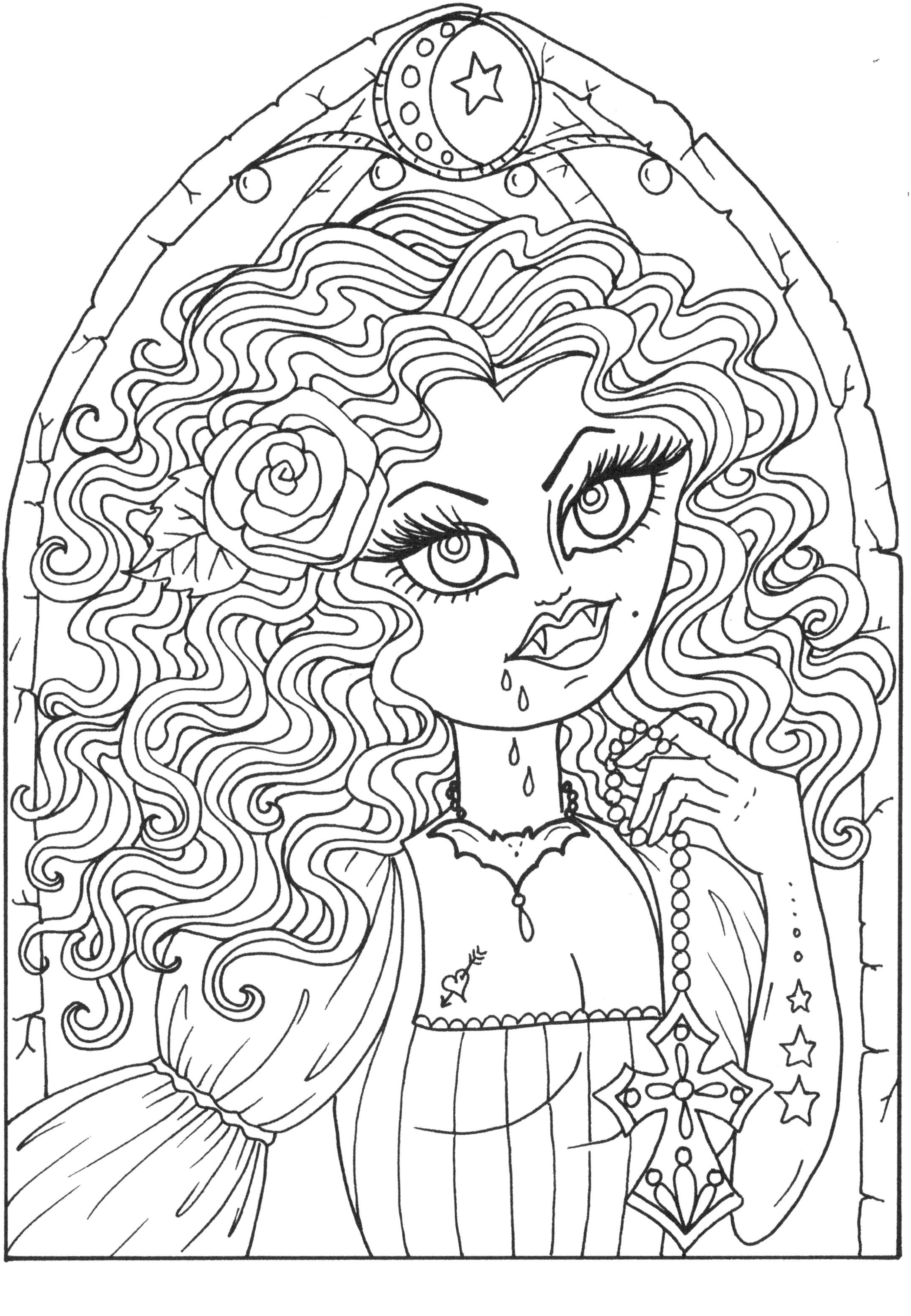

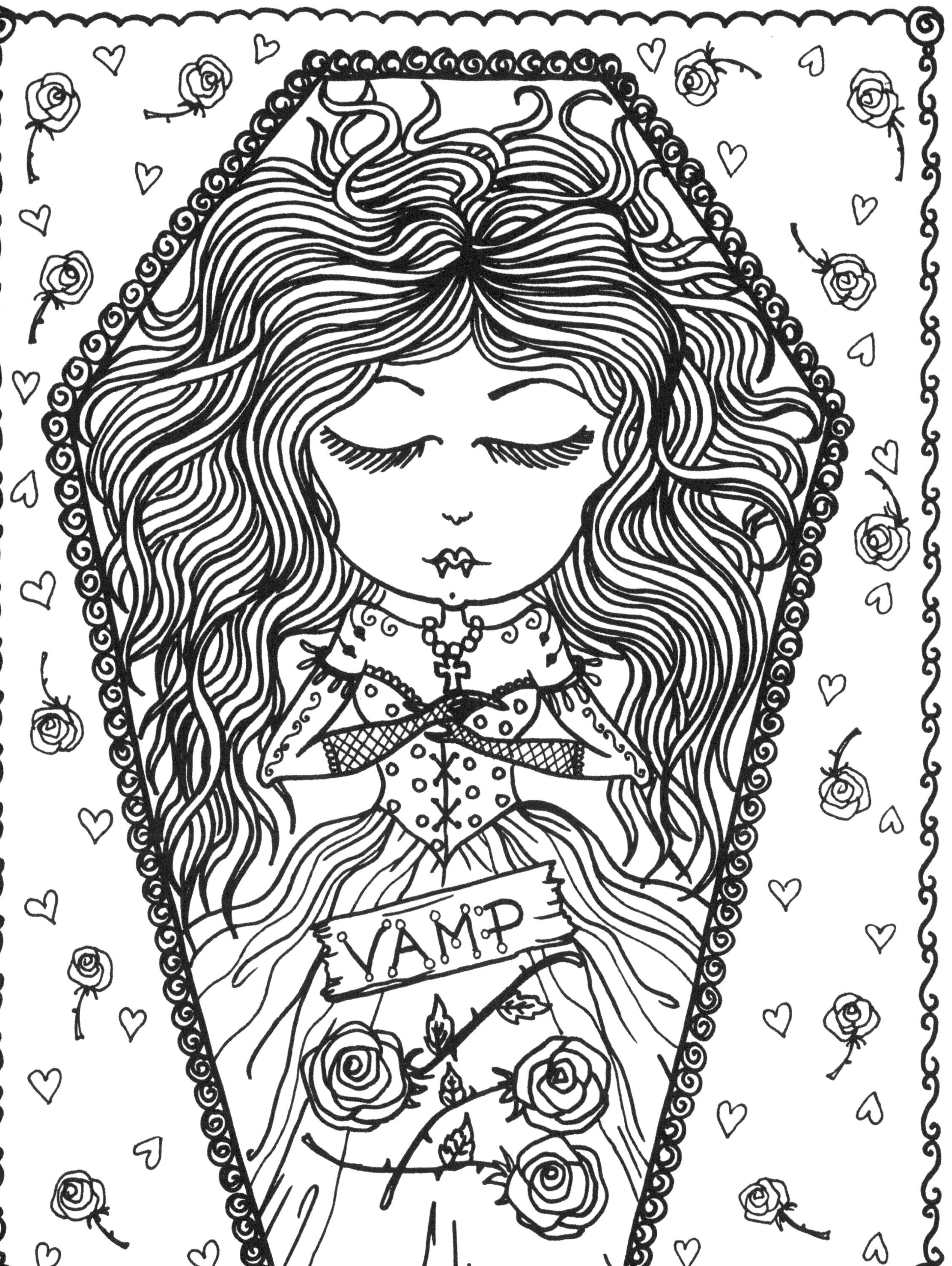
VAMP

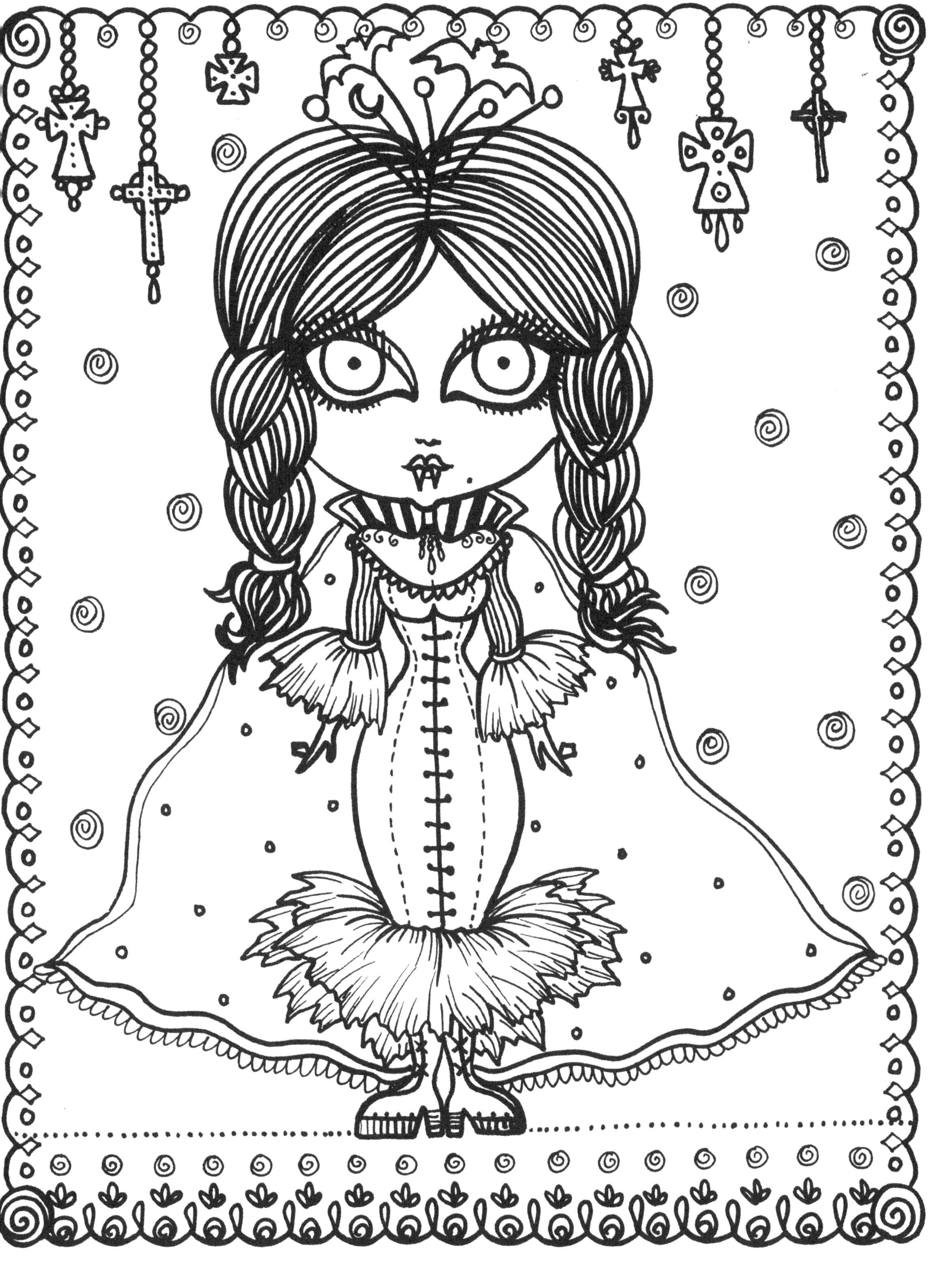

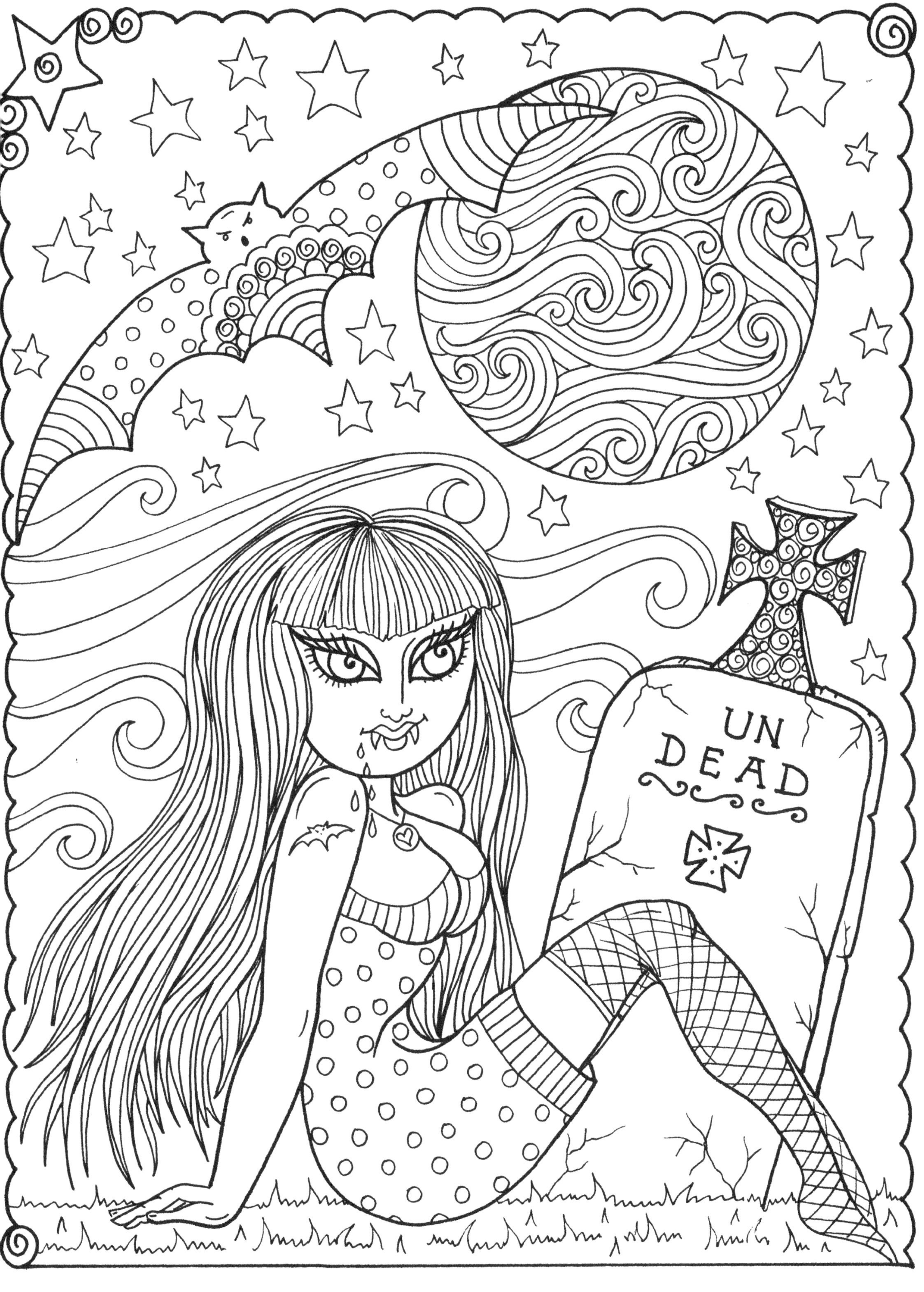
UN
DEAD

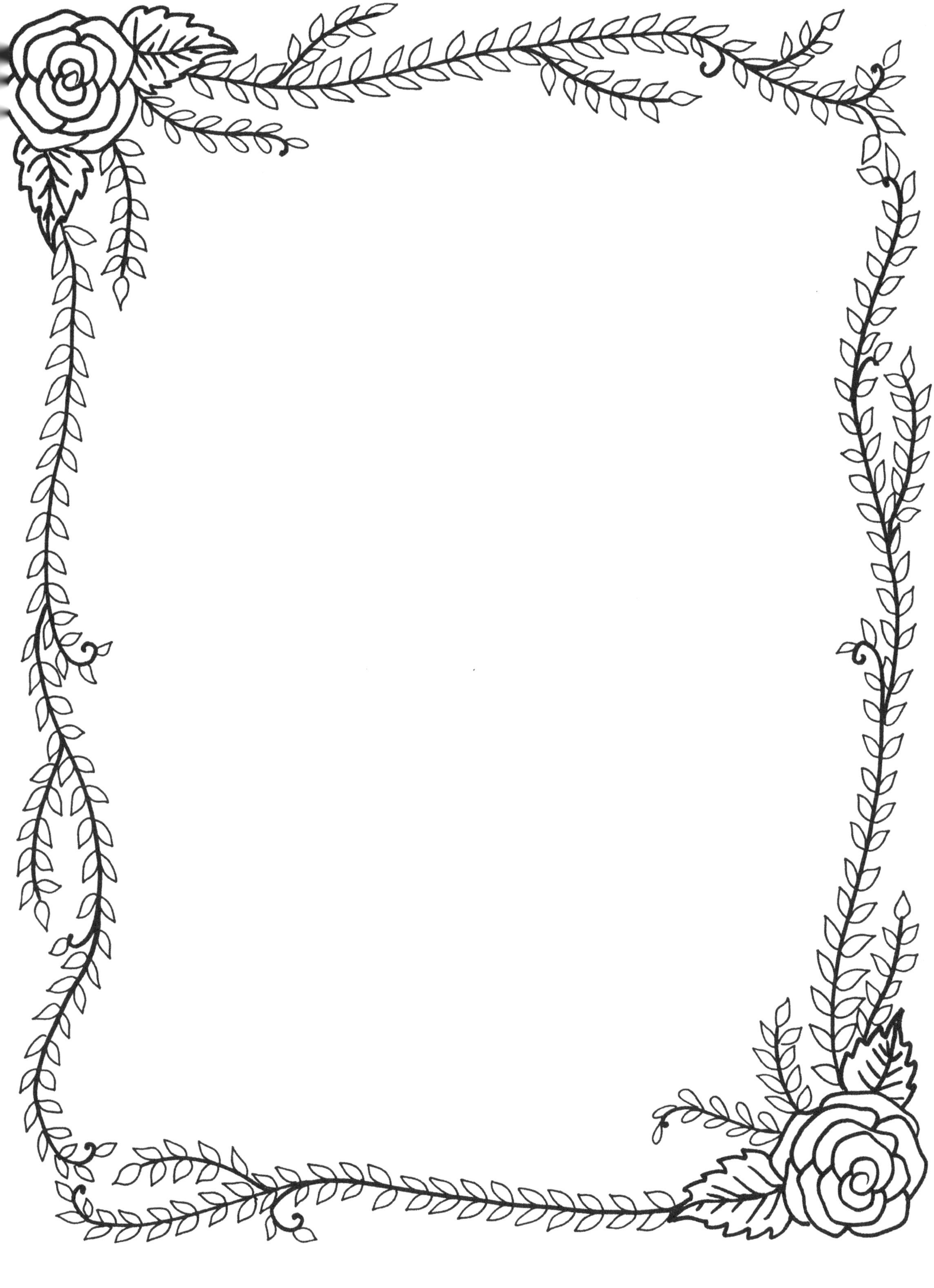

11146410R00026

Made in the USA
Monee, IL
06 September 2019